Let's Help Out

By Janine Amos and Annabel Spenceley

Consultant Rachael Underwood

alphabet
SOUP
an imprint of
WINDMILL BOOKS
New York

Published in the United States by Alphabet Soup, an imprint of Windmill Books, LLC

Windmill Books
303 Park Avenue South
Suite #1280
New York, NY 10010

U.S. publication copyright © 2010 Evans Brothers Limited
First North American Edition

Library of Congress Cataloging-in-Publication Data

Amos, Janine
        Let's help out! – 1st North American ed. / by Janine Amos and Annabel Spenceley.
    cm. – (Best behavior)
        Contents: Cleaning up – Helping Mom.
        Summary: Two brief stories demonstrate how to help out when you are with friends or at home.
        ISBN 978-1-60754-490-6 (lib.) – 978-1-60754-491-3 (pbk.)
978-1-60754-492-0 (6 pack)
        1. Helping behavior—Juvenile   [1. Helpfulness   2. Conduct of life]
I. Spenceley, Annabel   II. Title   III. Series
        177/.7—dc22

Manufactured in China

With thanks to: Gareth Boden, Aman Jutla, Samuel Mark, Emma and Abi Coomber, Lauren Griffiths.

Cleaning Up

It's time to clean up.

"Let's put everything back. Then we'll be able to find it tomorrow," says Gareth.

Sam puts the blocks
back in the box.

Aman puts the
clay in the tub.

Aman finds a block in the clay.
He takes it to Sam.

Sam has packed all
the blocks away.

Aman is still busy.
What could Sam do?

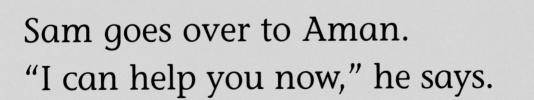

Sam goes over to Aman.
"I can help you now," he says.

They clean up the rest
of the clay together.

"We've finished!" says Sam.

"You worked together," says Gareth. "You helped each other."

Helping Mom

"Waah!" Abi is crying.

"She's been crying all night!"
sighs Mom.

"Do you want your rattle, Abi?" asks Mom.

"Nah!" says Abi.

"Do you want your drink, Abi?"
asks Mom.

"Nah!" says Abi.

"Brrr!" goes
the telephone.
"Waah!"
cries Abi.

"Oh, no!" sighs Mom.
How does Mom feel?

Lauren goes over to Abi.

She makes a funny face.

Abi smiles.

Lauren wiggles her fingers.

Abi laughs.

Lauren laughs too. "She's happy now," says Lauren.

"Thanks, Lauren,"
smiles Mom.

"You helped Abi –
and that helped me."

FOR FURTHER READING

INFORMATION BOOKS
Day, Eileen. *I'm Good at Helping.* Chicago: Heinemann, 2003.

Riehecky, Janet. *Cooperation.* Mankato, MN: Capstone Press, 2005.

FICTION
Brown, Marc. *Arthur Helps Out.* New York: L-B Kids, 2005.

AUTHOR BIO

Janine Amos has worked in publishing as an editor and author, and as a lecturer in education. Her interests are in personal growth and raising self-esteem, and she works with educators, child psychologists, and specialists in mediation. She has written more than fifty books for children. Many of her titles deal with first-time experiences and emotional health issues such as bullying, death, and divorce.

You can find more great fiction and nonfiction from Windmill Books at windmillbooks.com